50 INTERESTING F   WINE

A MUST- READ FOR WINE LOVERS

BLUMA BEE

50 Interesting Facts about Wine:

a must-read for wine lovers

Author: Bluma Bee

The author greatly appreciates you taking the time to read this work. Please leave a review wherever you bought the book.

To:

....

From:

....

Introduction

Inside this book is a collection of 50 interesting and funny facts about wine – the beverage that is older than our written history and even humanity. Wine has been around for as long as grape-bearing vines have existed, and it occurred naturally long before humans discovered the pleasurable effects of the alcohol contained in it and decided to cultivate the vine.

Because of wine, large territories have changed their rulers, and kings have put their reputations at stake. Wine tells the story of the land it comes from with the voice of the people who made it. Wine is ancient and hides many secrets, and every time you think you have finally figured it out, it will still surprise you. Worshiped and even considered mystical, wine has been the most frequently depicted beverage in the history of arts since ancient times, and Dionysius, the god of wine and theatre, is the youngest and the most cheerful god in the Greek pantheon.

Whether you're a wine enthusiast or just curious about the subject, this book is sure to delight and inform, with a wealth of fascinating facts and trivia about wine, its history, and its place in our culture.

1

Wine is generally considered to be fat-free and cholesterol-free and can be enjoyed in moderation as part of a healthy diet.

2

The sweeter the wine, the more calories it contains. This is because sweetness in wine comes from residual sugar, which is sugar that remains in the wine after fermentation.

3

It is estimated that there are more than 10,000 different varieties of wine in the world however, the main types vary between three (red, white and rosé) and five (red, white, rosé, sparkling and dessert), depending on whom you ask.

4

Bathing in red wine, also known as "*vinotherapy*", is an ancient practice supposedly introduced by Cleopatra, the Queen of Egypt. In present days, there is a spa in Japan that offers swimming in coffee, tea and ... wine. According to the owners, this is relaxing, fun and has anti-aging effect on your skin.

5

A good wine glass is thin, colorless, transparent, and unadorned, with a thin, long stem. It is filled to no more than a third of its volume and should be held firmly by grasping the lower part of the stem between your thumb and forefingers. The only reason we can hold the glass by the bowl is to warm a wine that is too cold.

6

The top rim of the wine glass, also known as the 'lip', is curved inwards to help concentrate the aroma of the wine when sniffing.

7

Chilling white wine or maybe Champagne without a fridge? Yes, it's possible. Put the bottle in a bucket full of ice and add salt. The rest is physics.

8

The proper way to preserve wine is by always keeping the bottles lying down. This way, the cork won't dry, shrink and eventually let air get in the bottle.

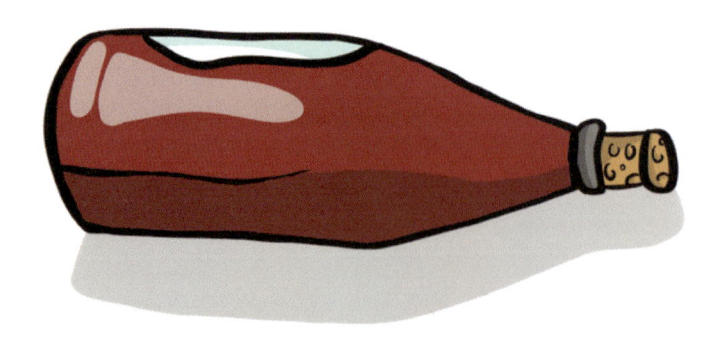

9

On average, it takes between 1kg and 1.2kg of grapes to make one bottle of wine. This is roughly 600 to 800 individual grapes.

10

Women generally make better wine testers than men due to their better sense of smell. After all, wine tasters essentially smell the wine.

11

Oenophobia – the fear or hatred of wine. Individuals with oenophobia may experience anxiety, panic, or discomfort in the presence of wine or even the thought of consuming it.

12

Mouthwash contains more alcohol than wine.

13

The oldest unopened bottle of wine can be found in a museum in Germany. It is estimated to be nearly 1700 years old.

14

Talking about old wine, did you know that the oldest wine cellar in the world can be found on board the Titanic wreck, and the bottles are still intact?

15

Over time red wines will lose colour while the whites will often darken and develop amber hues. In both cases, this is due to oxidation.

16

French oak is one of the most popular materials for making wine barrels. The average age of the trees when harvested is about 170 years.

17

'Sommelier' is the term describing a trained and knowledgeable wine professional responsible for the wine service in a restaurant – from the creation of the wine list to pairing with food and even servicing the restaurant guests.

18

In ancient times Greeks and Romans were very serious about wine and accordingly had a dedicated god of the grape harvest and merriment. To the Greeks, that was Dionysus, and to the Romans – Bacchus.

19

Wine tasting is a popular team-building event across the world and a nice way to spend part of your holiday. To properly enjoy it, however, you should not swallow the wine and spit it instead. Yes, it may seem wasteful, but in many cases, it is the only way to actually taste all the wines offered.

20

In the early days of ancient Rome, women were not allowed to drink wine. This was considered a crime, and even the death penalty was not uncommon. Thankfully, the laws were liberalised and the restriction removed.

21

Toasting is yet another thing that started in ancient Rome. The Romans would counter excessive acidity in wine by dropping a piece of toasted bread into their glass.

22

During the Middle Ages, the majority of the wine available was produced by monasteries and churches.

23

According to some sources, Vatican City consumes more wine per capita than any other country – 76 bottles per person annually.

24

Wine, especially red wine, is extremely rich in antioxidants. Just one glass contains the antioxidant equivalent of 7 glasses of orange juice or 20 glasses of apple juice. In moderation*, red wine has proven health benefits, reduces the risk of cardiovascular diseases and improves heart health in general.

* One glass a day

25

Tannin comes from 'tanna', the Old German word for oak or fir tree. The modern German word is Tannenbaum which also means Christmas tree. Tannins are responsible for the feeling of dryness in the mouth when drinking [mainly] red wine. You can determine whether a wine is high or low in tannins depending on how dry or moist your mouth feels.

26

Thanks to wine's popularity since ancient times, grapes are the most planted fruit in the world.

27

The largest wine producers in the world are Spain, France and Italy, followed by the USA and China.

28

The biggest producer of cork is Portugal; they produce about half of the world's cork wine stoppers. The material comes from cork oak trees which are so special that they have been protected by law since 1209.

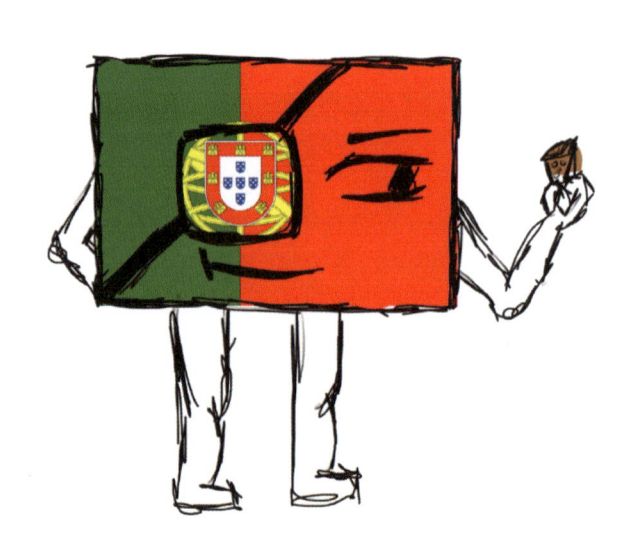

29

The harvest of cork is done by hand using a special type of axe. The process doesn't hurt the tree, which will regrow its bark in 8-9 years before the next harvest.

Did you know that the oldest cork oak tree on record is about 200 years old and has been harvested 20 times in its lifetime?

30

If there is such a thing as a universal rule for food and wine pairing, it is to pair foods and wines with the same or similar flavour intensity. An example of a good pairing is lobster and Chardonnay – both have similar bodies and complement each other very well.

31

King Charles received a vintage Aston Martin as a 21st birthday gift from his mother, the late Queen Elizabeth II. He has asked the Aston Martin engineers to find a new fuel type for the car to preserve the environment, and at present, the vehicle runs on a biofuel made of surplus English white wine mixed with whey.

The exact origins of the corkscrew are uncertain, as various devices and methods for extracting corks have been used throughout history. However, the earliest evidence of a corkscrew-like tool can be traced back to ancient civilizations such as the ancient Egyptians and Greeks.

The first known patent specifically for a corkscrew was granted to Reverend Samuel Henshall and the date of the patent was in 1795. Henshall's design featured a simple T-shaped handle and a sharp-pointed worm for extracting corks.

33

Richard Juhlin is a prominent Swedish Champagne author and holds the world record for blind tasting and successfully recognises 43 out of 50 Champagnes. For comparison, the runner-up guessed correctly only 4 of them.

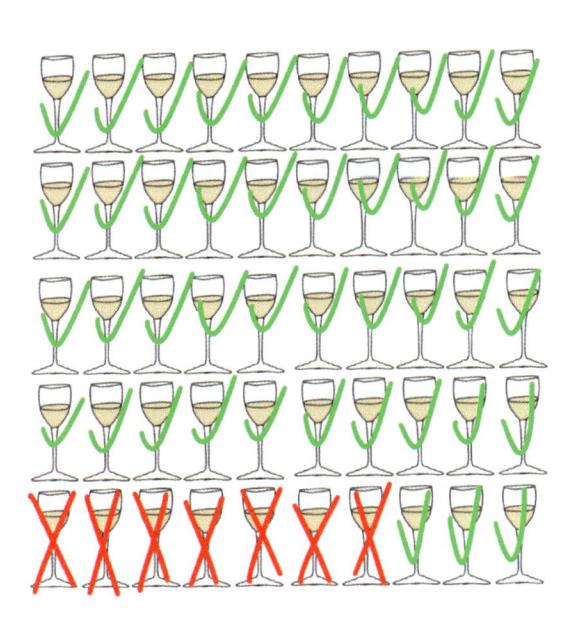

34

'*In vino veritas*' is a famous Roman saying, attributed to Pliny the Elder, that survived to modern days and means '*In wine there is truth*'.

35

The Hammurabi Codex is a 2.25m high stone pillar upon which a large collection of laws from ancient Mesopotamia is written. The section about wine is actually considered the oldest known wine law and includes provisions about yields, sales, prices and very strict punishments for violations of the provisions including, death by burning.

36

Wine and bubbles usually trigger only one association – Champagne. There is, however a claim that an Englishman, a 17th-century cider maker called Christopher Merrett, has discovered the secondary fermentation that puts bubbles into wine six years prior to the birth of Dom Perignon! Contentious, isn't it?

37

In 2016 a free 24 hours-a-day *'fontana del vino'* or wine fountain was opened in Abruzzo, Italy. The main goal was to support the Cammino di San Tommaso pilgrims, but anyone is welcome to visit the vineyard and have a free drink.

FREE WINE

38

USD558,000 – that much money was paid for the most expensive bottle of wine ever sold. It was a bottle of 1945 Romanee - Conti wine which is extremely rare, with only 600 bottles ever produced.

39

There are many wines featuring different animals on their labels. Their popularity is increasing and are collectively known as *'critter wines'*.

40

Beaujolais Nouveau is a famous young wine that is released every year on the third Thursday of November.

41

The period of USA history from 1920 to 1933 is known as the Prohibition. During that time, the production, import, transportation, sales and consumption of alcohol were not allowed. In order to survive, some American winemakers produced and sold completely legal wine bricks made of concentrated grape juice and helpfully added instructions on the label – *'after dissolving the brick in a gallon of water, do not place the liquid in a jug away in the cupboard for twenty-one days, because then it would turn into wine'.*

42

A *'coupe'* is a large, saucer-like champagne glass that has been modelled on Marie Antoinette's breast according to the legend. That's likely just a myth; however, a couple of famous, contemporary ladies have done exactly that – Kate Moss and Claudia Schiffer.

43

The alcohol content of wine can range from as low as 6% to as high as 20% or even more, but on average, sits around 12%.

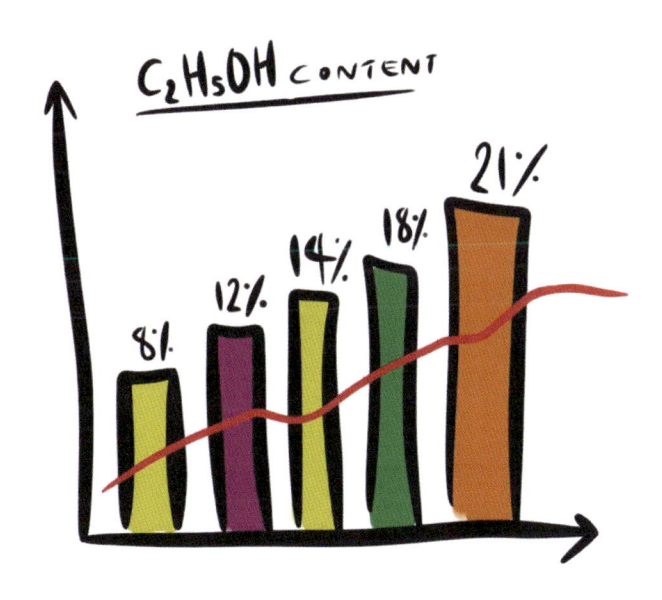

44

A very small (less than 1mm) aphid-like insect called *phylloxera* caused the so-called Great French Wine Blight in the 1860s when almost 70% of the wine vineyards in France were lost.

45

Wine is referenced multiple times in the Bible, and there are warnings about overconsumption.

46

The colour of wine comes from grape skins. So red wine can be made only from dark-skinned grapes, while white wine comes from both white grapes and their darker cousins but only if the skins are removed.

47

Moët & Chandon is a famous champagne.
Surprisingly, it is pronounced with a hard 't' and
not the typical French silent 't'.

48

Wine is said to be more complex than blood serum due to the high amount of organic chemical compounds it contains.

49

The dark green wine bottle was invented by Sir Kenelm Digby in the 1600's. Before that, wine was kept in goatskin bags.

50

Wine vernacular that makes you sound like an expert:

Complex – wine with many different flavours

Dense – wine with a high concentration of flavours and aroma

Crisp – fresh and acidic wine

Flamboyant – fruity wine

Elegant – light and well-balanced wine

Opulent – rich and bold wine

Earthy – a wine that smells of wet rock, slate, mushrooms

Age (of a bottle) – young (1-3 years), medium (3-5 years), mature (5+ years)

Flocculation – particles or sediment in wine. It's harmless but sounds awesome.

Vinosity – the characteristic body, colour and flavour of wine as it ages

If you enjoyed this book and would like to see more in the series, please leave a review on the Amazon page.

Other books by Bluma Bee:

Printed in Great Britain
by Amazon